Table of Contents

Dear Friends,

I am pleased to send you this report on the first-ever White House Summit on Community Colleges, which was held October 5, 2010 at the White House.

As we said in October, the White House summit was just the beginning of our national conversation to share the best practices to improve student outcomes at community colleges across the country. The Department of Education has continued that conversation by holding regional community college summits across the country focusing on topics that were discussed at the October summit. I am pleased to report that the four regional summits were a success, including rich discussions on how these institutions are contributing to the President's goal of making America the best and most educated country in the world by 2020 – and how they can learn from each other to continue to strive for better outcomes for their students. Each summit included community college presidents, students, full and part-time faculty, business leaders, education policy experts, state and federal lawmakers, the philanthropic community, and others.

The community college summits culminated at the end of April with the *Community College Virtual Symposium*, an online event that considered the following topics: bridge programs for low-skilled adults; alignment of secondary and postsecondary education; improved developmental education; and college-employer partnerships that promote curricular change. Participants logged on from across the country to engage in question and answer sessions with teams of scholars specialized in each topic.

I am proud of the work that so many of you have invested in this effort. Your participation and input is integral to the success of these discussions, and I know that many summit attendees have taken summit lessons back to your campuses. I look forward to working with you in the future.

Best,

Jill Biden, Ed.D.

White House Summit on Community Colleges
Mission Statement

To emphasize the role of community colleges in achieving the President's goal of making America the most educated country in the world by 2020.

To demonstrate that community colleges are critical partners in our efforts to prepare our graduates to lead the 21st century workforce.

To highlight the *Skills for America's Future* initiative, a new Gates Foundation program called Completion by Design, and the Aspen Prize for Community College Excellence.

Remarks by the President and Dr. Jill Biden at White House Summit on Community Colleges

DR. BIDEN: Hello. Good afternoon, and welcome to the first ever White House Summit on Community Colleges. I'm Jill Biden, and I'm proud to stand here today as a community college professor.

This is an historic and exciting opportunity for all of us in the community college world. For years I have said that community colleges are one of America's best-kept secrets. Well, with the President of the United States shining a light on us, I think that secret is out.

Today's summit is an important next step in our efforts to meet the President's goal of having the best-educated, most competitive workforce in the world by the end of this decade.

As we meet here today, families all across our country are struggling. We see that struggle firsthand in community colleges. We see people who are determined to build a better life for themselves and their families, no matter how hard it is. Today, community colleges are the largest, fastest-growing, most affordable segment of America's higher education system. For generations, these schools have been an option for many students who didn't have other options: recent immigrants, working adults, or students who could not afford or were not quite ready for a four-year institution.

Community colleges are uniquely American – places where anyone who walks through the door is one step closer to realizing the American Dream. These schools are flexible and innovative. For that reason, countries around the world are looking at community colleges as a model to increase workforce preparedness and college graduation among their own citizens.

Community colleges are uniquely positioned to provide the education and training that will prepare students for the jobs in the 21st century.

Schools are forming partnerships with businesses in their communities, ensuring that students are trained for jobs that need to be filled.

Getting Americans back to work is America's great challenge. And community colleges are critically important to preparing graduates for those jobs. We are here today because community colleges are entering a new day in America, and here's why: For more and more people, community colleges are the way to the future. They're giving real opportunity to students who otherwise wouldn't have it. They're giving hope to families who thought the American Dream was slipping away. They are equipping Americans with the skills and expertise that are relevant to the emerging jobs of the future. They're opening doors for the middle class at a time when the middle class has seen so many doors close to them.

As the President said, the nations that out-educate us today will out-compete us tomorrow. That is why he is committed to increasing the number of college graduates in America, so that we will once again lead the world in the percentage of our citizens with a college degree.

Community colleges are absolutely critical to reaching this goal, and to ensuring out country's economic prosperity in the future. That is why the President has also challenged all of us to graduate an additional 5 million community college graduates by 2020.

Reaching that goal will take the commitment of everyone in this room, and all of the hardworking community college leaders, faculty and students you represent.

Community college students and graduates across the country are working in jobs that will enable us to expand our green economy, provide Americans with the excellent health care they deserve, and rebuild our country's infrastructure.

These are the students like the ones I visited in their state-of-the-art radiology lab last spring at Delgado Community College in New Orleans. Or the woman I met who, after 16 years as a lab tech, came to Kingsborough Community College in New York for retraining, and graduated in nursing with a job offer waiting.

I meet students and learn about industry partnerships on every campus I visit that reinforce what we in this room know well: Community colleges are at the center of Americans' effort to educate our way to a better economy.

I've been a teacher for nearly three decades, and I have spent the past 17 years teaching at a community college. I know the power of community colleges to change lives.

I have seen the wisdom of Yeats who said that, "Education is not the filling of the pail, but the lighting of a fire." All of the teachers here today know the magic of lighting that fire in the soul of a student.

But as I work hard every day to inspire students, it is ultimately they who inspire me. I'm inspired by students who overcome significant odds just to show up, workers who have returned to school to improve their job prospects, mothers who juggle jobs and childcare while preparing for a new career, and students who spend two years at a community college before transferring to a four-year school.

At the President's request, I have visited community colleges around the country to see innovative job partnerships and creative student support programs. At each school, I hear stories about the perseverance of community college students to make a better life for themselves and their families – students like Albert, who inspire me and who I am thrilled to welcome here today. You're amazing, Albert.

The programs are different, the students are different, but the aspirations are the same. These students are working hard to get the training and education they need to make their lives better. They know that education can open the door to a world of new opportunities.

They are students like the mother who shared her experience with us on the White House website of working towards a degree while raising three children and straddling financial challenges. Now employed and the holder of a Bachelor's and a Master's degree, she wrote, "Community colleges didn't just change my life, they gave me my life."

Community colleges do that every day. With the support and the attention of the people in this room, we can serve more students and serve them better than ever.

Our challenge is not just to get students into college, but to keep them there and to graduate them faster with the skills they need to succeed in the American workforce. This is the moment for community colleges to shine.

Teaching is my life's work. I am grateful and tremendously proud to work with a President and Vice President who value that work. President Obama is committed to restoring the promise of the American education system. He recognizes the value of community colleges and is investing in them so that they are the best that they can be. His leadership is inspiring to all of us who believe that each and every American deserves the opportunity to realize his full potential.

I am honored to introduce a leader who shares our belief in the power of the community college, President Barack Obama.

THE PRESIDENT: Thank you. Thank you very much. Thank you so much. Thank you, everybody. Thank you very much. Everybody please have a seat. Thank you so much.

I want to acknowledge some of the folks who are here who are making an incredible contribution to this effort. First of all, our Secretary of Education, Arne Duncan, is here. Our Secretary of Labor, Hilda Solis, is here. Someone who cares deeply about our veterans and the education that they receive, our Chairman of the Joint Chiefs of Staff, Admiral Mike Mullen, and his wife, Ms. Mullen, are here. Representative Brett Guthrie, Republican of Kentucky, is in the house, and has been doing great work on this. And obviously I am thrilled to not only see Jill Biden here but also Albert Ojeda, who introduced Jill Biden, because I think the story he tells is representative of so many incredible stories all across the country.

I'm so grateful for Jill being willing to lead today's summit, first of all because she has to spend time putting up with Joe. And that's a big enough task. Then to take this one on, too, on behalf of the administration is extraordinarily significant. I do not think she's doing it for the administration. She's doing it because of the passion she has for community colleges.

Jill has devoted her life to education. As she said, she's been a teacher for nearly three decades, although you can't tell it by looking at her – a community college professor for 17 years. I want it on the record Jill is not playing hooky today. The only reason she's here is because her college president gave her permission to miss class. And this morning, between appearing on the Today Show, receiving briefings from her staff and hosting the summit, she was actually grading papers in her White House office.

So I think it's clear why I asked Jill to travel the country visiting community colleges – because, as she knows personally, these colleges are the unsung heroes of America's education system. They may not get the credit they deserve. They may not get the same resources as other schools. But they provide a gateway to millions of Americans to good jobs and a better life.

These are places where young people can continue their education without taking on a lot of debt. These are places where workers can gain new skills to move up in their careers. These are places where anyone with a desire to learn and to grow can take a chance on a brighter future for themselves and their families – whether that's a single mom, or a returning soldier, or an aspiring entrepreneur.

And community colleges aren't just the key to the future of their students. They're also one of the keys to the future of our country. We are in a global competition to lead in the growth industries of the 21st century. And that leadership depends on a well-educated, highly skilled workforce.

We know, for example, that in the coming years, jobs requiring at least an associate's degree are going to grow twice as fast as jobs that don't require college. We will not fill those jobs – or keep those jobs on our shores – without community colleges.

So it was no surprise when one of the main recommendations of my Economic Advisory Board – who I met with yesterday – was to expand education and job training. These are executives from some of America's top companies. Their businesses need a steady supply of people who can step into jobs involving a lot of technical knowledge and skill. They understand the importance of making sure we're preparing folks for the jobs of the future.

In fact, throughout our history, whenever we've faced economic challenges, we've responded by seeking new ways to harness the talents of our people. And that's one of the primary reasons that we have prospered. In the 19th century, we built public schools and land grant colleges – transforming not just education, but our entire economy. In the 20th century, we passed the G.I. Bill and invested in math and science – helping to unleash a wave of innovation that helped to forge the great American middle class.

But in recent years, we've failed to live up to this legacy, especially in higher education. In just a decade, we've fallen from first to ninth in the proportion of young people with college degrees. That not only represents a huge waste of potential; in the global marketplace it represents a threat to our position as the world's leading economy.

As far as I'm concerned, America does not play for second place, and we certainly don't play for ninth. So I've set a goal: By 2020, America will once again lead the world in producing college graduates. And I believe community colleges will play a huge part in meeting this goal, by producing an additional 5 million degrees and certificates in the next 10 years.

That's why last year I launched the American Graduation Initiative. I promised that we would end wasteful subsidies to big banks for student loans, and instead use that money to make college more affordable, and to make a historic investment in community colleges. And after a tough fight, we passed those reforms, and today we're using this money towards the interest of higher education in America.

And this is helping us modernize community colleges at a critical time – because many of these schools are under pressure to cut costs and to cap enrollments and scrap courses even as demand has soared. It's going to make it possible for colleges to better harness technology in the classroom and beyond. And it's going to promote reform, as colleges compete for funding by improving graduation rates, and matching courses to the needs of local businesses, and making sure that when a graduate is handed a diploma it means that she or he are ready for a career.

We're also helping students succeed by making college more affordable. So we've increased student aid by thousands of dollars. We've simplified the loan application process. And we're making it easier for students to pay back their loans by limiting payments to 10 percent of their income. But reaching the 2020 goal that I've set is not just going to depend on government. It also depends on educators and students doing their part. And it depends on businesses and non-for-profits working with colleges to connect students with jobs.

So that's why we're holding this summit. That's why I'm asking my Economic Advisory Board to reach out to employers across the country and come up with new ways for businesses and community colleges to work together. Based on this call to action, yesterday we announced a new partnership called Skills for America's Future. And the idea is simple: Businesses and community colleges work together to match the work in the classroom with the needs of the boardroom. And already, businesses from PG&E, to UTC, to the Gap have announced their support, as have business leaders like my friend Penny Pritzker, and the Aspen Institute's Walter Isaacson. I hope that the companies, schools and nonprofits that all of you lead will take part.

Today, we can also announce the Gates Foundation is starting a new five-year initiative to raise community college graduation rates. This is critically important because more than half of those who enter community colleges fail to either earn a two-year degree or transfer to a earn a four-year degree. So we want to thank Melinda Gates, who's here, for that terrific contribution. And the Aspen Institute and several leading foundations are launching a competitive prize for community college excellence. It's going to shine a spotlight on community colleges delivering truly exceptional results – places that often don't get a lot of attention, but make a tremendous difference in their students' lives.

So we're investing in community colleges. We're making college more affordable. And we're bringing together businesses, nonprofits and schools to train folks for the jobs of a new century. Now, all of this will help ensure that we continue to lead the global economy – but only if we maintain this commitment to education that's always been central to our success.

That's why I so strongly disagree with the economic plan that was released last week by the Republican leaders in Congress, which would actually cut education by 20 percent. It would reduce or eliminate financial aid for 8 million college students. And it would leave community colleges without the resources they need to meet the goals we've talked about today.

Instead, this money would help pay for a $700 billion tax cut that only 2 percent of the wealthiest Americans would ever see – an average of $100,000 for every millionaire and billionaire in the country. And that just doesn't make sense – not for students, not for our economy.

Think about it. China isn't slashing education by 20 percent right now. India is not slashing education by 20 percent. We are in a fight for the future – a fight that depends on education. And cutting aid for 8 million students, or scaling back our community – our commitment to community colleges, that's like unilaterally disarming our troops right as they head to the frontlines.

So we obviously have to get serious about our deficit. That's why, after decades of profligacy, my administration report pay-as-you-go rules, proposed a three-year freeze on non-security spending. That's why we've formed a bipartisan deficit reduction commission.

But what we can't do is fund tax cuts for those who don't need it by slashing education for those who do. There's a better way for us to do this. And I want to work together with everybody concerned – Republican and Democrat – to figure that out.

To use an expression familiar to those of you who are from the Midwest: You don't eat your seed corn. We can't accept less investment in our young people if our country is going to move forward. It would mean giving up on the promise of so many people who might not be able to pursue an education, like the millions of students at community colleges across this country.

So I just want to use as an example Derek Blumke, who's here today. Where's Derek? Right here. Derek spent six years in the Air Force, three deployments in the Afghan theater, putting his life at risk to keep this country safe. And when he returned, he started classes at his local community college in northern Michigan. Now, apparently, what I'm told is, he wasn't sure whether he was smart enough to do the work, and he also was concerned that he wouldn't get the support that he needed.

And he was wrong on both fronts. His professors not only helped him transition from the military – even as he continued to serve in the Michigan Air National Guard – but also helped him to earn his associate's degree with honors. Then he transferred to the University of Michigan – Go Blue – where he graduated just a few weeks ago. And while he was there, he co-founded Student Veterans of America to help returning veterans like himself. So congratulations, Derek.

Or we can look to the example set by Albert Ojeda, who just spoke to you. He didn't have any advantages in life – grew up in a tough neighborhood in Phoenix, lost his father to violence, lost his mother to prison. But that didn't stop him from pursuing an education. It didn't stop him from attending community college, become an honor student, become the first member of his family to graduate from college.

There are so many folks out there like Derek and Albert. And I think about the many community college students who've written letters to me or emails through whitehouse.gov about how important community college has been to them. One person said he had been laid off and decided to return to school after 17 years. And attending community college "literally helped save my life" – that's what he said. "I can not only see an associate's degree next year, but a new future filled with possibilities for the first time."

A new future filled with possibilities. That's why we're here today. That's the promise of an education not just for any one student, but for our entire country. And that's why it's so important that we work together on behalf of community colleges – and an education system that harnesses the talents and hard work of every single American.

So thank you for the incredible work that each and every one of you do out there in schools, business folks who are supporting these community colleges, the students who are doing so much to contribute to our country. Let's get busy. Thank you very much.

Breakout Session 1: Pathway to a Baccalaureate
Moderators: Under Secretary Martha Kanter & Roberto Rodriguez

"There are few things as fundamental to the American Dream or as essential for America's success as a good education." – President Barack Obama

Over the past three decades, the overall cost of higher education has increased more than four times the cost of living. Community college tuition, however, is far less than the cost of other institutions. The average annual tuition and fees at a community college are just over $2,500. The cost of attending a public 4-year college is over $7,000, and the cost of attending a private 4-year university averages around $22,500 – almost ten times the cost of attending a community college.

Given the rapidly-increasing costs, many middle-class families are turning to community colleges to provide the first two years of higher education, which can result in tens of thousands of dollars in savings over the course of their children's college experience. Some students also participate in dual enrollment programs while in high school, which can accelerate the time towards earning a degree and reduce the overall financial burden.

This session focused on ways to ease transfer from two-year to four-year institutions for those students who earn the first two years of a baccalaureate degree at a community college. Participants shared best practices and strategies for improving transfer, such as transparent articulation agreements, common course numbering, transfer Associate's degree partnerships, and guaranteed admission with junior status.

Recommendations

- Provide more information to students at the beginning of the process about which courses transfer and which count towards degrees
- Ensure dual enrollment courses transfer
- Create common course numbering systems in states, and perhaps nationally
- Implement "reverse transfer" by granting an Associate's degree after credit hours are completed, even if the student has transferred
- Be transparent about the full costs of tuition, and project college cost increases for prospective students
- Increase institutional consistency
- Establish clearly articulated pathways on the state level
- Institutionalize what works and shine a spotlight on high-impact practices
- Collect and use data thoughtfully
- Use technology to increase and improve services
- Create tools like collegefish.org to help students understand the transfer process
- Offer parent orientation
- Increase collaboration with K-12 and 4-year institutions
- Create internships for students to increase retention and persistence to transfer
- Jointly admit students to a community college and a university
- Institutionalize the faculty-to-faculty discussion

Breakout Session 2: Community College Completion
Moderators: Secretary Arne Duncan & Deputy Under Secretary James Kvaal

"In a single generation we've fallen from first to 12th in college graduation rates for young adults. And if we're serious about building a stronger economy and making sure we succeed in the 21st century, then the single most important step we can take is to make sure that every young person gets the best education possible — because countries that out-educate us today are going to out-compete us tomorrow."
– President Barack Obama

The days of being able to rely on a high school diploma to access a middle class life are over. Nearly 8 in10 new jobs in the next decade will require workforce training or higher education beyond high school. The economic imperative of higher education, for individuals and for our economy, is clear — yet we have fallen from the top in the world in college-educated young adults to 12th.

Community colleges are a vital part of our higher education system, enrolling 43% of all undergraduates and a disproportionate percentage of minority, non-traditional, older adult, low-income, working, parent, and first generation students — students who are particularly vulnerable to dropping out. Consider some completion numbers:

- Fewer than three in ten full time students pursuing a two-year degree graduate within three years — and part time students graduate at even lower rates.

- Less than half of community college students who enroll intending to earn a degree or transfer reach this goal in *six years*

According to the participants, there are many reasons for low completion. About 60% of community college students are referred to at least one developmental course. Less than a quarter of community college students who enroll in developmental education complete a degree or certificate within eight years. Students may be unable to navigate the financial aid process or to select appropriate courses, or schools may not offer the academic or social support students need. The reasons for low completion are many, but the fact remains that completion rates at community colleges are far too low.

This session focused on the need to increase completion and graduation rates at community colleges. Participants shared best practices and strategies for improving completion rates, particularly student support services, successful remedial education programs, accelerated time to degree, and credit for prior learning.

Recommendations

- Better communicate the value of a credential to help the public understand its purpose, quality and results
- Establish common metrics that measure progress and outcomes
- Establish block scheduling and directed choice to accelerate time to degree
- Consider how developmental education meets the needs of diverse learners
- Offer industry-run professional development for faculty
- Base state funding on completion, rather than enrollments
- Foster an institution-level culture of evidence-based decision making
- Be more aggressive about counseling
- Strengthen student support services
- Create stronger partnerships with industry to ensure work opportunities and job placement; increase teaching opportunities for business representatives
- Align graduation and entrance requirements between K-12 and community colleges
- Create high school dual-credit opportunities
- Use technology to increase capacity
- Increase the use of cohort-based education
- Grant Associate's degrees to students who have completed enough credits, even if they are seeking Bachelor's degrees (i.e. Project "Win-Win")
- Award credit for prior learning experiences
- Create transparent articulation agreements
- Link with President Obama's volunteer service corps to provide tutoring and High Touch for community college students; leverage the knowledge and resource of retirees

Breakout Session 3:
Affordability: Financial Aid to Community College Students
Moderators: Cecilia Rouse & Gene Sperling

"And that's why I'm absolutely committed to making sure that here in America, nobody is denied a college education, nobody is denied a chance to pursue their dreams, nobody is denied a chance to make the most of their lives just because they can't afford it."
– President Barack Obama

While community college tuition and fees are significantly less than those of four-year colleges, total costs are significant — particularly for low-income students. Community college students are much less likely, despite being disproportionately low-income, to apply for financial aid compared to students at four-year institutions. For those who do apply for aid, community college students are much more likely to have unmet needs after financial aid is awarded.

Financial aid systems were designed for what used to be called the "traditional" student — a full time, right-out-of-high-school student who is dependent upon his or her parents. This student is no longer the typical student — and certainly not at community colleges. Community college students are a much more diverse group, with the majority attending part-time and the majority working to support themselves and pay for school. 59% of full-time students work full-time and 40% of part-time students work full-time.

These statistics have serious implications for completion. Several recent studies by Public Agenda and the Community College Survey of Student Engagement found that most dropouts leave college because they have trouble going to school while working to support themselves and that finances were critical to their continuing enrollment in college.

This Administration has taken historic steps to increase affordability for our students. We have ended wasteful subsidies to banks that administer federal loans and have increased Pell Grants to make college more affordable for low-income students, made student loans more affordable through strengthened income-based repayment and public service loan-forgiveness, tripled the investments in tax credits for college expenses, and have made the financial aid process easier and faster to navigate by simplifying the FAFSA (Federal Application For Student Aid).

This session focused on the need to reduce obstacles to affordability for community college students. Participants shared best practices and strategies for increasing affordability, including further simplifying the financial aid process, improving awareness of financial aid among prospective and current students, using performance-based financial aid distribution to increase persistence, creating "emergency" funds for low-income students, and increasing financial support for students by leveraging federal, state, and local programs aimed at low-income individuals.

Recommendations

- Further simplify the financial aid process and forms
- Communicate the availability of federal aid and emphasize that aid can be used to cover the costs of attendance in addition to tuition and fees
- Create virtual financial aid offices, putting all federal aid information on the web and making it virtually accessible and language-accessible to all students – especially low-income students – so they can follow the process from beginning to end
- Provide the federal aid package for students as full-time, so they know how much they are eligible for whether they attend full- or part-time
- Urge employers to set consistent work schedules so students can attend classes consistently
- Make the federal aid application process more convenient by creating a one-stop-shop by locating admissions, financial aid, etc. all in one location
- Offer emergency grants to help students persist despite financial setbacks
- Leverage other federal resources for community college students
- Develop legislation to provide resources for colleges and universities to align more closely with K-12
- Attach maintenance-of-effort language to federal resources allocated to states
- Consolidate federal aid programs
- Extend the American Opportunity Tax Credit
- Build public-private partnerships in areas of outreach and financial literacy
- Rethink work disincentives with regard to Pell eligibility, such as the penalty for independent students to continue working
- Reevaluate aid for displaced workers

Breakout Session 4: Community Colleges in the 21ˢᵗ Century

Moderators: Melinda Gates & Melody Barnes

"…a new generation of innovations depends on a new generation of innovators."
— President Barack Obama

Community colleges meet students exactly "where they are," and today, with close to half of all undergraduate students in the United States enrolled in one of these institutions, they are serving the most diverse student body in history. Community colleges will need to innovate to meet the needs of the broad range of students in the 21ˢᵗ century: young and old, urban and rural, working learners, first-generation college students, students raising families, students hoping to transfer to a four-year school, and students seeking training to reenter the workforce. The range of students is matched by the range of needs in their communities. New businesses, like emerging green technologies, will require workers trained in new ways.

Technology is key to much of this change. On-line learning opens new possibilities for many students who might not otherwise be able to attend a community college.

This session focused on the ever-evolving role of community colleges and their need to remain flexible and adaptable to meet the needs of increasingly diverse 21ˢᵗ century students. Participants shared best practices and strategies for addressing the needs of 21ˢᵗ century learners, including technology-enabled tools that allow for more personalized instruction that identify problem areas as well as successful interventions, online courses and course delivery to better meet students' academic and timeline needs, and contextualized curricula that allow students at a variety of skill levels to prepare for a career.

Recommendations

- Communicate the value of a credential to inform people about its purpose, quality, and results
- Establish common metrics that measure progress and outcomes, disaggregated by student type
- Establish block scheduling and directed choice to accelerate time to degree
- Rethink developmental education to meet the needs of diverse learners
- Offer industry-run professional development for faculty
- Base state funding on completion, rather than enrollments
- Foster an institution-level culture of evidence-based decision making
- Be more directive about counseling
- Strengthen student support services
- Create stronger partnerships with industry to ensure work opportunities and job placement; increase teaching opportunities for business representatives
- Work with K-12 to ensure that high schools know what "college ready" means; align graduation and entrance requirements between K-12 and community colleges
- Work with high schools to create more dual-credit opportunities; provide college experience and college credit-bearing courses for high school students
- Use technology to increase capacity
- Increase the use of cohort-based education
- Award credit for prior learning experiences
- Create transparent articulation agreements
- Link with President Obama's volunteer service corps to provide tutoring for community college students; leverage the knowledge and resource of retirees

Breakout Session 5:
The Importance of Community Colleges to Veterans and Military Families
Moderators: Admiral Michael Mullen & Heather Higginbottom

"The contributions that our servicemen and women can make to this nation do not end when they take off that uniform. We owe a debt to all who serve. And when we repay that debt to those bravest Americans among us, then we are investing in our future – not just their future, but also the future of our own country"
– President Barack Obama

Community colleges support and strengthen the communities in which they are located by responding to the needs of the people, organizations, and employers who live and work in surrounding areas. Where there is a need to educate and build skills, community colleges respond swiftly and creatively to meet those needs. Many of these institutions have recognized that military families are a population with unique needs and challenges, and have responded by finding ways to educate and train members of our military and their spouses in their communities, across the country, and throughout the world. Securing an education and job training are top priorities for active duty service members, spouses and veterans, and community colleges are an attractive option for military families because of their affordability, program choice, convenience and flexibility of class offerings.

The military is already doing its part. In 2000, the Army created GoArmyEd, an online network that allows soldiers to take classes at twenty-nine colleges and universities, anywhere in the world, any time. GoArmyEd offers 24/7 support, tutoring, a virtual library, and college counseling. GoArmyEd's completion rate is 83%. Community colleges are also answering the call in a number of ways:

- 43% of all military undergraduates and 39% of those receiving veterans' education benefits have selected public, two-year institutions as the place to achieve their academic and career goals.
- Military members frequently list the opportunity to get a college education along with the funds to pay for it as one of their top three reasons for joining the military.
- For highly mobile military spouses, portable career training and the transferability of in-demand skills are critical to easing the transition to a new community.

This session focused on the role that community colleges play in supporting military families and veterans. Participants shared the best practices and strategies for increasing enrollment and persistence at community colleges for military families and veterans, including specialized services to help with transition to civilian life, financial assistance for military spouses to earn a credential in high-demand fields, providing opportunities to accumulate credits and earn a degree despite numerous moves, and granting academic credit for military training and service.

Recommendations

- Increase partnerships between community colleges, state and local labor departments, and industry to provide certificate training programs
- Offer more specialized training for veterans with PTSD
- Collect and analyze more institution-level data – from the most basic level of how many veterans are on campus
- Increase collaboration at the federal level (VA/DOD/ED) to better collect, understand, analyze, and disseminate data
- Increase vet-to-vet support
- Examine the effective use of GI Bill benefits
- Add a day to the TAP program when transitioning out to advise others in the same age group about the value of community colleges
- Increase VetSuccess on community college campuses
- Focus on special counseling, physical accommodation, and mental needs of those with traumatic brain injury
- Increase model partnerships like Camp Lejeune and Coastal Carolina Community College; military academic skills program where Marines get intensive math, English and reading skills to prepare for college
- Offer professional development for faculty who educate veterans

Breakout Session 6:
Industry-Community College Partnerships
Moderators: Secretary Hilda Solis & Penny Pritzker

"Now is the time to build a firmer, stronger foundation for growth that will not only withstand future economic storms, but one that helps us thrive and compete in a global economy. It's time to reform our community colleges so that they provide Americans of all ages a chance to learn the skills and knowledge necessary to compete for the jobs of the future."
- President Barack Obama

In an increasingly competitive world economy, America's economic strength depends upon the education and skills of its workers. In the coming years, jobs requiring at least an Associate's degree are projected to grow twice as fast as those requiring no college experience. And over the next decade, nearly 8 in 10 new jobs will require higher education and workforce training. To meet this need, President Obama set two national goals: by 2020, America will once again have the highest proportion of college graduates in the world, and community colleges will produce an additional five million graduates.

As the largest part of the nation's higher education system, community colleges enroll more than eight million students and are growing rapidly. They feature affordable tuition, open admission policies, flexible course schedules, convenient locations, and they are particularly important for students who are older, working, or need remedial classes. Community colleges also work with businesses, industry, labor, and government to create tailored training programs to meet economic needs like nursing, health information technology, advanced manufacturing, and green jobs.

This session focused on the need to strengthen collaboration between community colleges, labor, and employers to ensure that students complete with the skills employers need. Participants shared best practices and strategies for strengthening collaboration, including developing apprenticeship programs, working with industry to develop contextualized, modularized, and competency-based curricula, bridging the credit/noncredit divide in workforce training programs, providing credit for prior work experience based on industry competencies, and providing professional development opportunities for faculty and staff.

Recommendations

- Create formal partnerships and reciprocity between community colleges and businesses to ensure that the skills that are taught are the skills that are relevant
- Build evaluation into the partnership programs
- Offer courses to accommodate students' work schedules, and work with businesses so students' work schedules are consistent so they can complete their courses
- Be flexible about course delivery; delivery can be workplace-based, at odd hours, or online
- Create clear, accessible pathways from community-based and adult education training programs to community college certificate and degree programs
- Envision industry support beyond sending workers to community colleges for training; businesses can provide tuition support, internships, apprenticeships, faculty, and validation of curriculum as an ongoing partner with community colleges
- Integrate technical skills into remediation by tying courses to industry needs and making remediation more relevant for underprepared students
- Increase offerings of accredited training
- Require the participation of community colleges on workforce investment boards
- Recognize credit for prior learning and work experience
- Create a point of contact for businesses – including small businesses – at community colleges
- Outreach to small business owners to upgrade their own skills in addition to their employees' skills
- Create business incubators to help existing and prospective small business owners

White House Summit on Community Colleges
List of Participants

First Name	Last Name	Organization/Affiliation
Thomas	Aguilar	Illinois Central Community College/ Butler, IL
Ellen	Alberding	Joyce Foundation
Timothy	Albrecht	Community College of the Air Force
Leigh	Arsenault	Department of Education
Tom	Bailey	Community College Research Center
David	Baime	American Association of Community Colleges
Pamela	Baldwin	Craven Community College, NC
Melody	Barnes	Domestic Policy Council, The White House
Ann	Bartuska	Department of Agriculture
Lezli	Baskerville	National Association for Equal Opportunity in Higher Education
Chuck	Beck	Red Rocks Community College, CO
Jeremy	Begley	Trinidad State Junior College, CO
Helen	Benjamin	Contra Costa Community College District, CA
Thomas	Bennett	Parkland College, IL
Jared	Bernstein	Office of the Vice President
Katherine	Bibb Hubbard	Gates Foundation
Carrie	Billy	American Indian Higher Education Consortium
Zac	Bissonnette	University of Massachusetts Amherst, MA
Ron	Bloom	Department of the Treasury
Derek	Blumke	Student Veterans of America
George	Boggs	American Association of Community Colleges
Brian	Bosworth	Future Works
Noah	Brown	American Community College Trustees
Patricia	Buckley	Department of Commerce
Walter	Bumphus	American Association of Community Colleges
Pat	Callan	National Center for Public Policy and Higher Education
Ted	Carey	Monroe Community College, NY
Constance	Carroll	San Diego Community College District, CA
Cathy	Casserly	Carnegie Foundation for the Advancement of Teaching
Jean	Chatzky	NBC News
Frank	Chong	Department of Education
Chris	Christensen	Johnson County Community College, KS
Michelle	Cooper	Institute for Higher Education Policy
Catherine	Cornish	Anne Arundel Community College, MD
Georgia	Costello	Southwestern Illinois College, IL
Martha	Coven	Domestic Policy Council
Brenda	Dann Messier	Department of Education
Gerardo	de los Santos	League for Innovation in Community Colleges
Danielle	DiBello	Bergen Community College, NJ
Mike	Donilon	Office of the Vice President
Myrtle	Dorsey	Baton Rouge Community College District, LA
Charlene	Dukes	Prince George's County Community College, MD
Arne	Duncan	Department of Education
Charles	Earl	Washington State Board for Community and Tech Colleges, WA

White House Summit on Community Colleges
List of Participants

Karen	Elzey	Skills for America's Future
Peter	Ewell	National Center for Higher Education Management Systems
Cheryl	Feldman	District 1199C Training and Upgrading Fund
Keith	Ferguson	Department of Education
Richard	Floersch	McDonald's
Antonio	Flores	Hispanic Association of Colleges and Universities
Michael	Francesoni	UPS
Aaron	Fulkerson	Mindtouch
Jason	Furman	National Economic Council, The White House
Melinda	Gates	The Bill and Melinda Gates Foundation
Candace	Gingrich-Jones	Human Rights Campaign
Robert	Gordon	Office of Management and Budget, The White House
Bill	Green	Accenture/Business Round Table President
Joycelyn	Groot	Coastline Community College, CA
Jennifer	Gross Lara	Anne Arundel Community College, MD
Rep. Brett	Guthrie	Kentucky's 2nd District
Steve	Hanson	Renton Technical College, WA
Zelema	Harris	St. Louis Community College, MO
Thomas	Haun	AFL-CIO Building and Construction Trades Department
Marc	Herzog	Connecticut Board of Trustees, Community & Technical Colleges, CT
Heather	Higginbottom	Domestic Policy Council, The White House
Stacie	Hitt	Operation Diploma/Military Family Research Center
Sue	Hoppin	Blue Star Families
Cheryl	Hyman	Chicago City Colleges, IL
Jim	Jacobs	Macomb Community College, MI
Stan	Jones	Complete College America
Martha	Kanter	Department of Education
Jane	Karas	Flathead Valley Community College, MT
Richard	Kazis	Jobs for the Future
Patricia	Keir	Eastern Iowa Community College District, IA
Donna	Klein	Corporate Voices for Working Families
James	Kvaal	Department of Education
Jim	Leach	National Endowment for the Humanities
Jee Hang	Lee	American Community College Trustees
Paul	Lingenfelter	State Higher Education Executive Officers
Sue	Liu	Department of Education
Lisa	Maatz	American Association of University Women
Casey	Maliszewski	Raritan Valley Community College, NJ /Mount Holyoke College, NJ
Helen	Maliszewski	Parent of Casey Maliszewski
Eduardo	Marti	The City University of New York, NY
Elisabeth	Mason	Single Stop USA
Helen	McAlpine	J.F. Drake State Technical College, AL
Robert	Mendenhall	Western Governors University

White House Summit on Community Colleges
List of Participants

Jamie	Merisotis	Lumina Foundation
Deborah	Mullen	Military Families' Advocate
Michael	Mullen	Chairman of the Joint Chiefs of Staff
Janet	Napolitano	Department of Homeland Security
Anthony	Newberry	Jefferson Community & Technical College, KY
Jane	Oates	Department of Labor
Jon	Obergh	Department of Education
Eduardo	Ochoa	Department of Education
Albert	Ojeda	Estrella Mountain Community College-Maricopa Community College District/ASU, AZ
Eduardo	Padron	Miami-Dade Community College, FL
Eugenia	Paulus	North Hennepin Community College, MN
Janine	Pease	Fort Peck Community College, MT
Hilary	Pennington	The Bill and Melinda Gates Foundation
Penny	Pickett	Small Business Administration
Hal	Plotkin	Department of Education
Dina	Powell	Global Head of Corporate Engagement, Goldman Sachs
Penny	Pritzker	President's Economic Recovery Advisory Board
Jack	Quinn	Erie Community College, NY
Scott	Ralls	North Carolina Community Colleges, NC
Travis	Reindl	National Governors Association
Richard	Rhodes	El Paso Community College, TX
Jim	Rice	NEA
John	Rice	Great Basin College, NV
Michael	Rice	Ivy Tech Community College, IN
Mike	Richards	College of Southern Nevada, NV
Roberto	Rodriguez	Domestic Policy Council, The White House
Jim	Rose	Wyoming Community College Commission, WY
Simon	Rosenberg	NDN Think Tank
Cecilia	Rouse	Council of Economic Advisors, The White House
Kay	Ryan	Former Poet Laureate
Eva	Sage Gavin	GAP
Sandra	Schroeder	American Federation of Teachers
Jane	Schulman	Laguardia Community College, NY
James	Selbe	Hopkinsville Community College, KY
Peter	Sercer	Midlands Technical College, SC
Karen	Sitnick	Office of Employment Development
David	Skorton	President, Cornell University, NY
Doug	Smith	Department of Homeland Security
Randy	Smith	Rural Community College Alliance
Zakiya	Smith	Department of Education
Kathy	Snead	Servicemembers Opportunity Colleges
Tom	Snyder	Ivy Tech Community College, IN
Louis	Soares	Center for American Progress
Hilda	Solis	Department of Labor
Bob	Songer	Lifelong Learning Branch, Camp Lejeune, NC
Gene	Sperling	Council of Economic Advisors, The White House

White House Summit on Community Colleges
List of Participants

Suzanne	Sublette	Madison Area Technical College, WI
Kenneth	Svensson	Parent of Mark Svensson
Mark	Svensson	SUNY-Rockland Community College, NY
Elizabeth	Swanson	Pritzker Foundation
John	Sygielski	Mount Hood Community College, OR
Wiliam	Taggart	Federal Student Aid, Department of Education
Robert	Templin	Northern Virginia Community College, VA
Bridget	Terry Long	Harvard University
Candace	Thille	Carnegie Mellon University
Linda	Thor	Foothill DeAnza Community College District, CA
Jerry Sue	Thornton	Cuyahoga Community College, OH
Frank	Toda	Columbia Gorge Community College, OR
Van	Ton-Quinlivan	PG&E
Mary	Wakefield	Department of Health and Human Services
Mike	Walcoff	Department of Veterans Affairs
Ross	Wiener	Aspen Institute
Ronald	Williams	The College Board
Katharine	Winograd	Central New Mexico Community College, NM

Next Steps

Community College Regional Summits

The October Summit was the beginning of this important conversation. While the Department of Education recognizes the role that the Federal Government plays in higher education, we also know that states and institutions will be central to meeting the President's 2020 goal. Secretary of Education Arne Duncan has been working with interested Governors to support State-led completion efforts. We have built on the work of the White House summit by identifying ways to identify best institutional practices to increase completion at community colleges through a series of four regional community college summits held in February, March and April of 2011. In addition, the Department of Education hosted a Community College Virtual Symposium on April 27th of 2011:

February 28   **Community College of Philadelphia, Philadelphia, PA**

March 9   **Lone Star Community College District, Houston, TX**

March 23   **Ivy Tech Community College, Indianapolis, IN**

April 15   **San Diego Community College District, San Diego, CA**

The regional summits were one-day events with 150 participants selected to ensure representation from community colleges, businesses, philanthropy, labor, state and local government, and students. Each summit had breakout sessions on a variety of topics, and a detailed focus on each of the following areas: serving military personnel, their families and veterans; supporting the transition of low-skilled adults into community college; rethinking developmental education; and creating sustainable business partnerships.

A summary of the proceedings, telecasts, and notes on the panel presentations, breakout sessions and report-outs from all four summits are posted on the Department of Education's website, and have been shared with the community college community.

You can find more information about the regional summits on the Office of Vocational and Adult Education website at the link below.

http://www2.ed.gov/about/offices/list/ovae/pi/cclo/index.html

Next Steps

Community College Virtual Symposium

The Department of Education conducted a *Community College Virtual Symposium* in April at Montgomery College in Rockville, Maryland. The Symposium presented and discussed the preliminary findings of four issue brief topics including: promoting college and career readiness among low-skilled adults; serving students who are not college-ready - reinventing developmental education; articulation and transfer from secondary and postsecondary institutions with special focus on career and technical education; integrating industry driven competencies in education and training through employer engagement. The Symposium provided institutional leaders with specific ideas about action steps they can take and information about models and resources they can access.

A live audience attended the Symposium at the host site, but the Symposium was primarily designed for a national webcast.

You can find more information about the community college virtual symposium on the Office of Vocational and Adult Education website at the link below.

http://www2.ed.gov/about/offices/list/ovae/pi/cclo/meetings.html